Wishing Leaves

Favourite Nature Poems
By Wayne Visser

Third Edition

I0170023

Third paperback edition published in 2016 by
Kaleidoscope Futures, London, UK.

First and second paperback editions published
in 2010 by Your P.O.D. Ltd and in 2012 by
Wayne Visser. First and second electronic
edition published in 2011 by Wayne Visser and
in 2016 by Kaleidoscope Futures.

Cover photography and design by Wayne Visser.
Cover photograph of the author by Indira
Kartallozi.

Printing and distribution by Lulu.com.

ISBN 978-1-908875-26-6

Dedication

Inspired by nature, an oblation to life in all
its shades, this is an ode to the grand force
that is at once our creator, nurturer,
sustainer and destroyer.

Dedicated to Mom and Dad, who kindled
my love of nature, instilled respect for all
life and encouraged my environmental
interests from a tender young age.

Fiction Books by Wayne Visser

I Am An African: Favourite Africa Poems

Wishing Leaves: Favourite Nature Poems

Seize the Day: Favourite Inspirational
Poems

String, Donuts, Bubbles and Me: Favourite
Philosophical Poems

African Dream: Inspiring Words & Images
from the Luminous Continent

Icarus: Favourite Love Poems

Life in Transit: Favourite Travel & Tribute
Poems

Non-fiction Books by Wayne Visser

Beyond Reasonable Greed

South Africa: Reasons to Believe

Corporate Citizenship in Africa

Business Frontiers

The A to Z of Corporate Social
Responsibility

Making A Difference

Landmarks for Sustainability

The Top 50 Sustainability Books

The World Guide to CSR

The Age of Responsibility

The Quest for Sustainable Business

Corporate Sustainability & Responsibility

CSR 2.0

Disrupting the Future

This is Tomorrow

Sustainable Frontiers

The CSR International Research
Compendium

The World Guide to Sustainable Enterprise

About the Author

Wayne Visser was born in Zimbabwe and
has lived most of his life in South Africa
and the UK. He is a writer, academic, social
entrepreneur, professional speaker and
amateur artist.

Wayne has a deep love for nature, its
beauty and diversity, which is given voice
through this collection. His views on the
natural world are best summed up in his
own words:

I cherish
The gardens of the world
and the world of gardens
The hope of seeds and the seeds of hope
The growth of buds and the buds of growth
The life of trees and the tree of life
The joy of flowers and the flower of joy
The goodness of fruit
and the fruit of goodness
The magic of butterflies
and the butterfly of magic
The love of the gardener
and the gardener of love

Website: www.waynevisser.com

Email: wayne@waynevisser.com

Contents

Wishing Leaves

We sat upon the bench that autumn night
And basked beneath the moon's cool silver
light,
While waves of traffic lapped the park's
green shore
And squirrel's rushed to fill their acorn
store.

A gust of wind set off a whispered sigh
Among the trees that leaned against the
sky;
We listened hard to catch their secret words
Between the chirping chatter of the birds.

Then as we turned our faces to the moon –
Our hands entwined; our hearts in sync, in
tune –
We felt the fingers of the silken breeze
And made our wishes on the falling leaves.

I Think I Was A Tree Once

I think I was a tree once,
A long, long time ago.
It doesn't help to question;
It's something I just know.

I feel it when I'm swaying,
While gentle breezes blow,
And when my feet are rooted,
I feel the earth below

I fall with leaves of autumn -
My time for letting go;
I sleep with dreams of winter
Beneath the fallen snow;
I blossom in the springtime -
An iridescent show;
I bask in rays of summer -
Filled with an inner glow.

I feel the sap within me,
While silently it flows,
And as I reach for sunlight,
I feel my spirit grows.

I walk among the forest
When I am most alone
And there, among my kindred,
I know that I've come home.

Kaleidoscope

Kaleidoscope colours carpet the ground –
A palette of yellow, red, green and brown.
Splashes of sunshine transform the
　　　prosaic;
Layers of leaf-paint reveal the mosaic.

A blustery breeze
Tugs at the trees;
Somehow they know
They must let go
With spiral flutters
As autumn mutters
And makes her bed
With tear-leaves shed.

Her blanket soon fades, leached pale by the cold

Her leaves disappear, consumed by the mould

She falls into slumber and dreaming, she yearns

For the colours of spring – the kaleidoscope turns.

A Future Worth Fighting For

"This is war!"
So my son tells me
And my daughter agrees
But I have some questions
I don't really like wars
Or making enemies
So tell me ...

If this is war
What are we fighting for?

We are fighting for the earth:
For the birds of the air
And the fish of the sea
For the sick in the villages
And the hungry in the cities

If this is war
Where are the battlefields?

The planet is our battlefield:
The smoky plains of the skies
And the murky streams of the oceans
The burning lungs of the forests
And the aching hearts of the people

If this is war
Who is the enemy?

The enemy is our separation:
Hiding behind fences of politics
And sheltering in dugouts of religion
Lurking under shadows of economics
And camouflaged in masks of progress

If this is war
Who are our allies?

Our allies are ordinary people:
The luminous tribes of the South
And the caring villages of the North
The rising tides in the East
And the changing winds in the West

If this is war
What are the weapons?

The weapons are our faith:
Our fortress of courage to hope
And our bedrock of belief in justice
Our wellspring of creativity for solutions
And our fire of passion for change

If this is war
Where is the battle?

The battle is where you are:
Around the fires of your homesteads
And the tables of your boardrooms
In the aisles of your supermarkets
And on the wires of your networks

If this is war
Who are the losers?

The losers are prejudice and vice:
For judgement is the father of fear
And power is the mother of pride
For hatred is the child of ignorance
And greed is the orphan of isolation

If this is war
Who are the winners?

The winners are life and love:
For diversity flourishes with freedom
And hope blooms with compassion
For development spreads with peace
And purpose calls to us all

This is war then!
So my children tell me
And I for one believe them
I still don't like the talk of battles
But I think they are right
The future – their future –
Is worth fighting for

Gentle Storm

Upon a clear and frosty autumn morn,
I chanced upon a gentle swelling storm.
No lightening flashed across the azure sky;
No thunder rolled and all the ground was
      dry;
No rain or snow, no whisper of a breeze,
And yet a shower fell beneath the trees.

Swooping and swirling,
Drifting and diving,
Wafting and weaving,
Floating and flirting.

And while the leaf-drops all around me fell,
I stood entranced by nature's silent spell.
Kaleidoscopic colours filled the air
And, mesmerised, I could only stare:
A light-and-motion dance that left me high;
A tempest raging, quiet as a sigh.

How the Mighty Have Fallen

All through the sapling days
Of dark and dappling haze,
You stretched for skies
Of perfect blue.

Up to refracted rays
All through protracted days,
You reached for highs
And so you grew.

Until you broke the night;
At last, unyoked the light.
Like living prose,
You stood so tall.

Until the gale's grey might
Ripped through your sail's green height
And, as you rose,
So you did fall.

Grey and Gold

The paths are spread with carpets grey and
gold
And walls are hung with quilts of green and
red;
The air is laced with clouds of frosty cold
And bridges hung with webs of silver
thread.

The sun is slow to raise its sleepy head
And parks are strewn with beads of
diamond drops;
The night is long with scattered stars ahead
And fields are bare with stubble-bearded
crops.

The trees are flushed with moods of
swirling change
And skies are strung with faith on migrant
wings;
The land is brushed with nature's palette
range

And hearts are warm with hope that
  autumn brings.

Stone Walls

Tectonic forces heave and strain;
Volcanic cones spew fiery rain.
Molten lava cools to rock
And Gaia reels in aftershock.

The master crafter we call Time
Begins to shape, shift and define –
With tools of wind and sun and rain –
A landscape from the barren plain.

Then stone by stone, with human hand,
Great circles spread across the land –
Like ancient scripts: a story told
Of sacred life in times of old.

Soon people gather on the scene
To dig and blast and mine the seam.
From crumbling quarries hewed of stone,
They carve rough blocks to make their
        home.

Then rising up around each place,
Stone walls dissect the open space
And leave behind a patchwork quilt
Of hamlets, towns and cities built.

Monet's Dream

The leaves are falling to the ground
I caught one as it fell today
And Monet's dream lay all around

I watched it fall without a sound
The green of summer's gone away
As leaves are falling to the ground

My hands were outstretched, heaven-bound
The leaf was dancing, swish and sway
While Monet's dream lay all around

It fell with grace, I was spellbound
As if the earth had bowed to pray
And leaves were falling to the ground

It landed soft, my hands closed round
As if I'd caught a golden ray
While Monet's dream lay all around

Inside me, something lost was found
It touched me more than words can say
While leaves were falling to the ground
And Monet's dream lay all around.

Misty Woods

Shrouded trees and autumn mulch
Shining leaves and sponge-mud squelch
Spotted toadstools, crimson red
Sparkling jewels on spiders' thread

A million drops wrung from the sky
A million drops from leaves on high
A million drops splash to the earth
A million drops to quench her thirst

Through cloudy woods on smoky trails
With glistening cloaks and wispy veils
Two figures drift on through the haze
Two lovers in the misty maze

Earth Invocation

Earth needs no saving by you or by me
For nature transcends our will to survive
With branches and roots spread wide on
      life's tree

The green of the land, the blue of the sea
The cycle of seasons always revive
Earth needs no saving by you or by me

Progress misleads in the name of the free
For nature is meant to flourish and thrive
With branches and roots spread wide on
      life's tree

The shade of the woods, the flow of the
      streams
The greatest of climbs and deepest of dives
Earth needs no saving by you or by me

We shoot for the stars as far as we see

And remake the world as we search and
    strive
With branches and roots spread wide on
    life's tree

The planet won't need another decree
Only our passion to keep life alive
Earth needs no saving by you or by me
With branches and roots spread wide on
    life's tree.

Forest Invocation

The forests are burning
The skies filled with smoke
The climate is churning
The children still choke

Let's end all this madness
Let's halt our demise
Let's fight for our jungles
Let's clean up our skies

The forests are falling
The land cleared for oil
The green frog is calling
The life's in the soil

Let's end the destruction
Let's strengthen our pleas
Let's fight for our future
Let's care for our trees

The forests are dying
The cancer is greed
The creatures are crying
The rivers still bleed

Let's end the excuses
Let's act to survive
Let's call on our leaders
Let's keep trees alive

The forests are living
The lungs of the earth
The trees keep on giving
The worlds' in rebirth

Let's take up the challenge
Let's march for a change
Let's seed revolution
Let's replant the grange

The forests are spreading
The lesson is learned

The dead skin is shedding
The hope has returned

Let's dance for the woodland
Let's sing for the grove
Let's praise for the jungle
Let's rhyme as we rove

The forests are thriving
The chorus is loud
The feeling's enlivening
The old trees stand proud

Let's remake this Eden
Let's rise from our knees
Let's bring back our forests
Let's celebrate trees.

Haiku: Beauty

Bare trees on still pond
Stark silhouettes, reflecting
Beauty, unconscious.

Ideas of Winter

Clouds drift
In billowing embrace –
Reassuringly grey,
Unexpectedly white,
Wrapping me up
And tucking me in,
Safe under duvet skies,
Content on verdant pillows,
Happily watching
Short days
Curl in on themselves,
Longing for rest,
In search of dreaming,
While puce clouds
Weigh the possibility
Of dropping their ballast
And watering
Ideas of winter.

Come Rain, Come

Come, rain, come!
Swirl with the mists of intrigue,
Like the ethereal wisp of whistles,
Shrouded with mystery
And enchanting.

Come, rain, come!
Patter with the kiss of butterflies,
Like the gentle blend of voices,
Infused with salve
And healing.

Come, rain, come!
Fall with the gift of life,
Like the soothing tap of marimbas,
Blended with tonic
And quenching.

Come, rain, come!
Pour with the pulse of ages,
Like the rhythmic beat of drums,
Stirred with emotion
And invigorating.

Come, rain, come!
Storm with the cry of battle,
Like the mighty clash of cymbals,
Consumed with passion
And transforming.

Come, rain, come!
Arch with the bow of promise,
Like the haunting wail of saxophones,
Imbued with colour
And inspiring.

Fog

What was it about the fog
That day
That so enchanted me?

As I tumbled out of my front door,
The path before me –
Usually clear into the distance –
Had disappeared;
Swallowed up
In a great white cloud.

I waded through the mist
To the bridge across the river,
Which flowed out of nothing
Into nowhere.
The intrepid ducks and boats
Were on shrouded journeys
Into the unknown,
Perhaps to the very edge
Of the world.

I walked through the park,
Fascinated
As murky phantasms emerged
And melted into thick air,
Like wraiths in the netherworld
Gliding between lost and found,
Hovering around gloomy lampposts,
Searching for signs
To uncertainty.

And as I walked through the wispy veil,
Trees rose up to greet me,
Reaching out with dripping fingers,
Enfolding me
In the damp blanket of myopia;
Tucking me in
With whispers of letting go
And trusting the unseen.

That whole day
The fog lingered,
Blotting out the glaring sun,
Opening an invisible portal
Into the realm of shades,
Where beauty drifts
In rainbows of grey
And wisdom beckons
At the blurry fringes
Of consciousness.

First Snow

It didn't snow on Christmas Day,
No jingle bells nor Santa's sleigh,
No gifts to wash my cares away,
No wings to lift my feet of clay.

But two days later snowflakes fell
And broke the curse of sadness spell;
Its beauty coaxed me from my shell
And dowsed my flames of private hell.

The bitter freeze began to break
Like shards upon the frozen lake;
The icy chill of my heartache
Began to thaw and dissipate.

The numbing pain of things gone wrong
In this past year will soon be gone;
Upon the breeze, the robins' song
As days get longer from now on.

Storm

Vapour clashes in the vortex,
Like brewing broth in caldron black;
Lightning lashes the horizon,
Like splintered shards of broken sky;
Thunder crashes through the silence,
Like devilled drums of godly war;
Sheet-rain splashes in the mud-dust,
Like horses hooves on battle ground;
Sunlight flashes through the storm-veil,
Like soothing spells to tame the waves;
Sodden ashes quench the spirit,
Like phoenix flames that rise on wing.

Winter Song

Crunching boots like music beat,
Globs of light on misty street,
Puffs of breath like smoky lace,
Dripping nose on frozen face.

Frosted leaves like festive cake,
Shards of ice on glassy lake,
Silver sun like shining moon,
Twilight stars come out too soon.

Cosy rooms like thermal hugs,
Steaming soup in favourite mugs,
Calls to shop like ringing gong:
Hum along to winter song.

Rain

Before the rain:
Expectation hangs in the air,
A shadow moves across the sun
And cools the baking sand;
Thirst grows acute.

Then it rains:
Petals and arms open wide,
A haze drifts through the streets
And soaks the glistening leaves;
Desire is quenched.

After the rain:
Relief floods over the earth,
A grey sky soothes the senses
And refreshes tired minds;
Life begins anew.

Zen Garden

Still pond
Koi swim
Trees bow
Fronds coil

Mind reflects
Thoughts ripple
Time bends
Space unfurls

Water trickles
Frogs hop
Flowers bloom
Leaves rustle

Meaning flows
Ideas leap
Joy smiles
Insight whispers

Paths connect
Bridges reach
Stones stand
Crystals shine

Feet explore
Hands touch
Eyes close
Focus distils

Dragons appear
Coins glint
Lanterns glow
Statues watch
Birds twitter

Shadows swirl
Wishes sparkle
Hope kindles
Wisdom lingers
Harmony sings

Chimes sound   Ideals echo
Benches beckon   Beauty poses
Silence speaks   Peace settles

Tea steams   Love quenches
Cat purrs   Affection spills
Child laughs   Spirit soars
Gardener nods   Zen grows

Giant White Hand

Between aspiring, cloud-laced mountain
   peaks,
The ancient Giant White Hand reaches over
   –

Its outstretched fingers, cool and
   crystalline,
Grasping at rock and tree in the valley
   below;
Its cracked fingernails stained translucent
   blue,
Scratching at the gritty surface of soaking
   ground –
Shrouded in silence.

Crack!
A raucous, rumbling avalanche of icy flesh
   flakes away,
Cascading over jagged knuckle and smooth
   snowy skin.
Then silence again.

But for the drip, drip, dripping

Of pure sweat from some enormous
invisible effort,

Tarrying a while in turquoise pools,

Slithering away in swift-flowing streams,

Racing down rocky channels in churning
rapids,

Leaping off clinging cliffs in thunderous
waterfalls,

Freely frothing over into fathomless fjords,

Then silently melting into its maternal
source.

Until one day, it is born again from
heavenly seed –

New blood to pulse through the veins

Of the next Giant White Hand

To hold our Earth orb in its palm.

Serenity

Calm turquoise waters and white tufted
      skies
Red fiery sea crabs with knobbly stalk eyes
Black sea iguanas with arched horny
      spines
Blue-footed boobies that plummet and dive

Time drifts and eddies, space sweeps and
      curls
My body unhinges, my mind gently swirls

Gold crescent beaches and green mangrove
      trees
Acrobat frigates that twist on the breeze
Sky-dreaming cactuses rise from the ash
Shy silver fishes shimmy and flash

Days stretch and unfurl, nights pulse and
      pause
My heart finds its rhythm, my soul lifts and
      soars

Cool soothing drizzle and grey lapping
waves

A vigilant pelican watches and preys

Fresh footprints fade as the lunar-tide
churns

A white-tipped shark ghosts and glides as it
turns

Hopes swell and teeter, dreams froth and
spray

Serenity lingers as I go on my way.

The Tree-Keepers

The other day, on Hampstead Heath
While mist lay shrouded like a wreath
I chanced upon some tree-keepers
With leaves above and mulch beneath

Now tree-keepers, I must explain,
Are much the same as bee-keepers –
Though less about the drowsy smoke
And more about the high-slung rope;
Less about the honey wax
And more about the pruning axe;
Less about the buzzing bees
And more about the tufted trees –
So ... not so much, it must be said,
Like bee-keepers at all.

But tree-keepers, I will admit,
Are almost like chimney-sweepers –
Just less about the charcoal dust
And more about the leafy rust;
Less about the fiery chutes
And more about the twisted roots;
Less about the blackened bricks
And more about the wayward sticks –
So ... not so much, in actual fact,
Like chimney-sweepers at all.

Still, tree-keepers, I'm sure it's true,
Are pretty much like fire-eaters –
But less about the searing spark
And more about the ailing bark;
Less about the showmanship
And more about the budding slip;
Less about the more absurd
And more about the nesting bird –
So ... not so much, if truth be told,
Like fire-eaters at all.

In actual fact, the tree-keepers
Are nothing like the night-sleepers
Or keyhole-peepers or canyon-leapers;
Not a bit like money cheaters
Or egg-white-beaters or candy-treaters;
Not even like crawly-creepers,
Let alone grim-hooded-reapers –
No ... not so much, despite their rhyme,
Like any '–eepers' after all.

Rather, those strangers on that day
On Hampstead Heath, I'd have to say,
Were nothing more and nothing less
Than keepers of wise Nature's way.

Skylight

Sky of mauve
Clouds alight
Pink and peach
Pure delight!

Dawn

Sunrise scatters rays of dawn
Until the seeds take root and spawn
New chances to create and thrive
Reviving calls to seek and strive
Inscribed upon the code of life
Survival skills of care and strife
Evoked as darkness turns to light.

My Spring

My boots are thud, thud, thudding
Like a beat upon the street,
While blooms are bud, bud, budding
On the trees still without leaves.

My heart is beat, beat, beating
Without rest within my chest,
While birds are tweet, tweet, tweeting
On the ledges and in hedges.

My Spring is come, come, coming;
Soon her song will sing along,
With days of sun, sun, sunning
On the rise across my skies.

Daffodil

Rising from your winter sleep,
Stretching leafy limbs of green,
Yawning yellow wisps of dream.

Behind frozen curtains peep,
Waving in the bracing breeze,
Nodding at the naked trees.

Whispering secrets that you keep,
Teasing out the timid sun,
Promising that spring is come.

Garden of Hope

I remember so clearly the barren crater,
Gouged from the ground in our yard,
Dusty with sand and jagged with rubble –
A porta-pool grave of plastic and wire.

Who had the foresight, the vision, the faith
To see in its midst, the garden?
Who had the hope, the courage in life
To dream of flowers and streams?

The reality was bleak in its ghastly form,
But the future was all for creating;
And now we see the triumphant seed
Of imagination nurtured by labour.

The hole has been covered, moulded and
     planted
And is bursting blooms with a colourful
     blaze;
The water, once sterile, now flows to a pond
Where family gathers and darting fish play.

This is the star in the darkness of night,
The jewel in the mountain of rock;
This is my glade of peace and tranquillity,
My inspiration – my garden of hope.

Little Flower

Gorgeous little flower
From far off distant shores,
Trapped in your finest hour,
You bloom each time I pause.

You shine in all you glory
With petals spring unfurled,
And hid inside this story,
You travel round the world.

Pressed between these pages,
I see your smiling face;
Your beauty through the ages
Now helps me mark my place.

I Am Ocean

i am ocean
i am wave
i am current
i am tide

i am vapour
i am cloud
i am droplet
i am rain

i am puddle
i am pool
i am lagoon
i am lake

i am river
i am flood
i am rapid
i am falls

i am motion

i am still

i am cycle

i am flow

i am essence

i am source

i am vital

i am life.

Trooping the Colour

There is a hidden army on the rise –
A covert operation, underground –
And listen as you might for frosty sighs,
They plot their takeover without a sound.

But see that splash of colour through the
      trees?
That's the purple coat of an advance scout;
And see that swish of motion in the breeze?
That's a bright helmet of gold sticking out.

You may not hear the drum of marching
      boots,
Or see the glory flags of tomorrow,
But mark where bright sentinels put down
      roots,
For there, iridescent troops will follow.

When the Lilies Bloom

Our Mother Earth, with flaming fever,
Our Father Sky, with floods of tears,
Our Brother Sun, in smoke enshrouded,
Our Sister Moon, toils with the tides.

The fiery dawn sees its reflection,
The searing noontime is ablaze,
The bleeding dusk is cut with torrents,
The midnight feels the waters rise.

Men and women dress for battle,
Armed with bucket, barrow, hose;
Young and aged grasp at safety,
Cling to photos, memories, toys.

War cries echo across besieged land,
Amidst the roar and smoke and grime;
Some are taken hostage, prisoner
On island rooftops, in fiery cells.

The choked skies, the drenched horizon,
Pulse and throb with rotor-winged birds
Who quench the flames and throw a lifeline,
Like glistening angels of mercy hovering.

At last, the firestorm exhausts its fury,
The smoky veil in the heavens is rent;
At last, the tempest lashes its last blow,
The dark cloud cloak is cast aside.

From scattered ashes, so bleak, so desolate,
Bright green buds, like a phoenix, burst
          forth;
From silted plains, so washed out and
          forlorn,
Brave new buildings, like flowers, will rise.

From glories of summer, to tragedies of
    autumn –

Many leaves fallen, many lives lost;

With winter – lamenting and struggles for
    survival;

With spring – healing and a new lease of
    life.

As with the rainbow (an ancient covenant
    divine),

This time of renewal and rebirth will come;

The promise radiates from the ashes and
    mud –

This sacred moment, when the lilies bloom.

Witness to a Kill

I'm witness to a massacre –
Unwitting and unknowing –
Upon my tiny balcony
Where fledgling life was growing.

A pigeon chose our shielded nook
To make her nest and lay her eggs;
Two squawking chicks had soon appeared,
All skin and spikes, all beaks and legs.

Our proud new mum was diligent
As back and forth she fussed and flew;
She fed them well, they sprouted wings,
Their motley feathers grew.

We used to wake and listen to
Their urgent, hungry cries;
Who knew that tragedy would strike
And leave us heaving saddened sighs?

It happened on a lunchtime break:
I ventured out to take a look,
And as I stepped out on the ledge
I frightened off a jet-black rook.

I froze and gazed in disbelief
At feathers scattered all around;
Yet still I hoped that I was wrong,
Until I saw blood on the ground.

The two grey chicks were ripped to shreds,
Just guts and gore were left to show;
Their carcasses were hollowed out,
Their brave new wings had grown too slow.

Right in that moment, raged welled up –
A bitter bile of blackbird hate;
All I could think in my distress
Was that I'd come too late … too late.

I cleared the scene as best I could –
Put carnage into plastic bags;
It felt undignified as they
Went in the bin like shredded rags.

Later that day, the mum returned –
I watched to see what she would do;
She looked ... and looked ... it broke my
        heart –
It's like she knew, I'm sure she knew.

The rook has come back several times;
I do not harbour ill will still,
For Nature's kind and Nature's cruel
And I – a witness to a kill.

A Bug's Life

If I could speak *butterfly*,
I think that I would giggle;
And if I walked *caterpillar*,
I'm sure that I would wiggle.

If I could hear *dragonfly*,
I think that I'd be fickle;
And if I felt *ladybird*,
I'm sure that it would tickle.

If I could smell *honeybee*,
I think that I would shimmer;
And if I tasted *moonlit-moth*,
I'm sure my world would glimmer.

Kingdom of Magic

Sacred world of fairies and elves,
Angels of light, and weavers of spells;
Friends of the earth, of the sky and the sea,
Charming our hopes, alive in our dreams.

Perhaps one day, when we truly believe,
We'll wake from our slumber, and there you
    will be:
A kingdom of magic and wonder and gleam
Larger than life; dream of our dreams.

Switch!
(Earth Day)

Switch off the lights
Turn off the plugs
Click ... flick ... click ...

Slow down the clocks
Calm down the rush
Tick ... tock ... tick ...

Let the dark enfold you
Let the stillness hold you
And hear the earth
Breathe a sigh of relief

Let the stress escape you
Let the moment take you
And feel the moon
Change a tide of belief

Strike up a match
Light up a candle
Flicker ... flutter ... flicker ...

Watch as your thoughts dance
Wait as your mind grows
Quicker ... quieter ... quicker ...

Let the hour unwind you
Let the meaning find you
And sense the touch
Of invisible hands

Let the rhythm shift you
Let the song uplift you
And feel the heartbeat
Of connected lands

Lighten your tread
Brighten your path
Step ... stop ... step ...

Act for the child

Care for our home

Switch ... shine ... switch!

The Park

A time for reflecting and healing
For reconnecting and dreaming
A time out, to search within
To find rhyme if not reason

A space for thinking and writing
For tending to wounds from fighting
A space odyssey, in one place
In which to touch mystery's face.

Summer Sunshine

The sun shone today
And the whole world came out to play:

Boys in flip-flops half-heartedly chasing
    frisbees
And bees buzzing dreamily over dazzling
    flowers;
Slow-motion rowers gliding under weeping
    willows
And swans drifting lazily in their rippled
    wake.

Girls in bikinis slow-roasting like chickens
And students with unopened files on their
    laps;
Entwined couples whispering under shady
    trees
And friends in tangled knots on vermillion
    grass.

Mums in sun hats making bubbling
    conversation

And overheated kids popping like popcorn;

Engrossed bookworms sitting on portal
    benches

And swaying tramps thirsty for a drop of
    kindness.

Dads in shades kicking footballs, beer in
    hand,

And panting dogs on the neighbourhood
    gossip trail;

Joggers and bikers glistening with beaded
    satisfaction

And me, watching and waiting, writing and
    wondering.

Today, summer unfurled

And playing was the way of the world.

Dandelion

I've seen you in the pavement cracks
And growing by the tin-roof shacks;
You lace the hills and edge the dales
And cast your net of feathered veils.

I've heard a girl say you were smoke
And there's a boy thought you were broke;
Your face I've touched, so soft and light,
And with each wish you've taken flight.

I've seen you ride upon the breeze
And there are insects that you tease,
But with each journey that you make
You spread the joy of give-and-take.

I've heard you called a simple weed
And much besides, but don't take heed;
So much in nature's whole and true,
But nothing's perfect quite like you.

Let Bells Ring Out

There are bells for weddings, bells for births
And bells for calls to prayer;
There are bells for mourning, bells for mirth
And bells for freedom's dare.

There are bells for fire, bells for floods
And bells for threatened shores;
There are bells for silence, bells that thud
And bells for music scores.

So why no bells for Nature's ways,
No bells for dusk or dawn?
Why no bells for dying days,
No bells for breaking morn?

And why no bells for summer sun,
No bells for winter moon?
Why no bells when autumn's come,
No bells for springtime bloom?

Let bells ring out for living things,
All creatures small and great;
Let bells ring out: with beating wings,
Our messengers of fate.

Let bells ring out from mountain peaks
And toll from valleys low;
Let bells ring out: Creation speaks
And all the world should know.

Unwanted Gift*

Water is a gift of life,
But generous Nature
Gave too much this time.

Her Christmas gift
Was never asked for,
Was never on anybody's wish list.

It was a fatal surprise
That should never have been sent,
Never have been opened.

But now it is too late,
For the gift cannot be returned,
Cannot be refunded or exchanged.

At the post-Christmas sale,
Life is going cheap
In the bargain bins of Asia.

Now in a sinister twist
Of the true spirit of Christmas,
We have a second chance to give.

Water is a gift of death
And the greedy Reaper
Took too much this time.

* Remembering the victims of the Asian Tsunami
of 26 December 2004

Thistle-Puffs

The thistle-puffs upon the gentle breeze
Shimmer in the sun like fairies' wings,
As seedling thoughts adrift in minds at
      ease.

The rustle sounds among the swaying trees
Whisper of the joy that summer brings,
With thistle-puffs upon the gentle breeze.

The flowers flirt and dreamy insects tease,
Sipping sap and dancing coded rings,
As seedling thoughts adrift in minds at
      ease.

The chirping lilt of nature's symphonies
Harmonise with songs the season sings,
Of thistle-puffs upon the gentle breeze.

The swirling tides upon the restless seas

Conjure waves of wild imaginings,

Like seedling thoughts adrift in minds at
ease.

The feathered clouds appear as heaven's
keys,

Portal to a world of secret things,

Like thistle-puffs upon the gentle breeze

And seedling thoughts adrift in minds at
ease.

Shapeshifting

A regal king with golden locks
Commands with thunderous roar;
The earth and all its kin are scarred
By bloodstained tooth and claw.
His form is sleek, his flight is swift,
His destiny is clear:
To dominate the open plains
And rule the land through fear.

There is another, no less noble,
No less strong or bold;
Survivor through the ages past,
All climes of hot and cold.
Her shifting shape floats by with grace,
Like misty clouds so rare:
She drifts across the dusty land
With gentle rumbling care.

Fire Flood

Dewy drops of sun-soaked rays
Become a steady shower,
Building to a lashing storm
Of searing, scorching power.

Puddle heat of rippled sheen
Sparking in the light;
Spraying mists of smoky cloud
That scale to towering height.

Winds whip up a fiery tide
That crashes wave on wave
On shore of tinder grass and pine,
All drowned beneath the blaze.

Valleys swell with molten streams
That snake with eerie glow;
Cascading falls of liquid flame
Down mountain gorges flow.

At last the tempest's fury ends
With wounds of sooty mud;
Black scars of chars can heal to green -
Survivor of the fire flood.

Oh, To Be A Cloud

Oh, to be a cloud,
Adrift in deep blue skies,
Without a care,
With wisp and flair,
No whos or whats or whys.

Oh, to be a cloud,
Above the world so high,
To smile and tear,
To disappear,
To flit and flut and fly.

Oh, to be a cloud,
Windswept from shore to shore,
Without a home
To call your own,
No polestar to implore.

Oh, to be a cloud,
A blocker of the sun,
To rage and roar,
To rain and pour,
To always spoil the fun.

Oh, to be a cloud,
Of any shape you please,
To bend the glow
Into a bow,
To dance and daze and tease.

Oh, to be a cloud,
A bridge for heaven's gulf,
I'd be arcane,
But then again,
I'd rather be myself.

Great Fathers of the Forest

Tall and noble you stand,
Members of a sacred council,
Silent in wise consensus.

I remember your rooted past,
See your swaying present,
Imagine your reaching future.

I sense your patient pulse,
Touch your fibrous skin,
Embrace your ample girth.

You and the earthworms alone
Are the quiet survivors
Of a lost world of giants.

You are the guardians of time,
The keepers of ancient wisdom,
The elders of our earthly tribe.

What would you teach us
If we had the humility
To sit at your feet and listen?

What secret knowledge
About surviving and thriving
And growing old gracefully?

What patient lessons
About thinking big, starting small
And aiming high?

I am a comforted babe,
Rocked to sleep in the cradle
Of your gentle ways.

I am a curious child,
Scaling the heights of possibility
In your outstretched boughs.

And when I leave
To pursue my impatient life,
I carry you in my heart.

And when I die,
You will be my ancestral guides –
Great Fathers of the Forest.

Still Pond

There is a secret place on Hampstead Heath
Where ancient trees surround a pond of
     peace
Where ducks and moorhens strut and
     preen
Where a silent heron stands guard, unseen

The seasons lap like tides upon the trees
Budding and blooming and scattering
     leaves
While the pond breathes its living ebb and
     flow
From winter's frost-glass to summer's fire-
     glow

I visit there to find my resting place
A calm eye amidst life's swirling pace
I visit there to renew my earthly bond
To find myself, reflected, in the still pond.

The Spirit of Nature

The Nature of Spirit ...

In the flowers –

the patterns of consciousness;

In the waters –

the ebb and flow of energy;

In the trees –

the cycle of birth, life and death;

In the mountains –

the landscape on which we choose life's
      paths

                  ... Is the Spirit of Nature.

The Waves

The waves, the waves are rolling in
Rolling in, building and breaking
Rolling in, swelling and swaying
Like an endless dance of to and fro
An endless march of letting go

The sea, the sea is restless still
Restless still, foaming and frothing
Restless still, tugging and teasing
Like an endless rhyme of ebb and flow
An endless ode of undertow

The waves, the waves in endless dance
An endless dance of letting go
An endless rhyme of undertow
Like a swaying march of to and fro
A teasing ode of ebb and flow

The surf, the surf is calling me
Calling me, rumbling and roaring

Calling me, crashing and cresting
Like an endless song of high and low
An endless voice from long ago

The tide, the tide is coming in
Coming in, pushing and pulling
Coming in, bubbling and breathing
Like an endless drawing of the bow
An endless wheel of reap and sow

The waves, the waves in endless song
An endless song from long ago
An endless drawing, reap and sow
Like a cresting voice of high and low
A breathing wheel, a flexing bow

The sand, the sand is shining gold
Shining gold, soaking and shifting
Shining gold, blowing and burning
Like an endless sky of sunset glows
An endless dream of sculpted rows

The waves, the waves are tumbling in
Tumbling in, chasing and churning
Tumbling in, streaking and spraying
Like an endless rhythm, fast and slow
An endless gift of art on show

The sea, the surf, the tide, the sand
Restless, calling, coming, shining
Frothing, roaring, pulling, shifting
Like a rolling wave of gifts on show
A tumbling wave of dreams to know.

Earth, Air, Fire, Water

I am Earth:
Grounded and mounded
And moulded in clay
Secret and shrouded
And hidden from day

Womb am I:
Life is seeded and sprouted
And spread out in green
I am fertile and febrile –
The guardian unseen

I am Air:
Wispy and misty
And swirling in space
Fleeting and flirting
And moving with grace

Breath am I:
Life is shaped and spoken
And scattered in white
I am ethereal, inspiring –
The guardian of flight

I am Water:
Flowing and knowing
And fresh with surprise
Snaking and slaking
And shifting disguise

Thirst am I:
Life is suckled and sated
And swaddled in blue
I am replenishing, forgiving –
The guardian of new

I am Fire:
Burning and yearning
And purging the night
Forging and flashing
And shedding all light

Heat am I:
Life is sparked and stoked
And flame-licked in gold
I am passion, transcendence
The guardian of soul

We are Earth, we are Air
We are Water and Fire
And the mission we share
Is to quench life's desire

The message we bring
Is the wisdom we keep:
That we four merge to one
In the love that you seek.

Penguin Dreams

Out of the dreamy ocean blue
A penguin glides into my view
With simple grace and body sleek
Wave-surfing every trough and peak

I long to know her secret ways
I watch her as she dives and plays
I see her battling stormy seas
And basking in the summer breeze

The day she lands upon my shore
She seems more lovely than before
With sparking eyes that glint of fun
She glistens in the winter sun

Her beauty takes my breath away
I only hope that she can stay
So much to share, to give and take
I'm dreaming that I'll never wake.

Caged

An animal caged may be well cared for
Protected and pampered, admired and fed
But can what's gained ever make up for
What's lost if the spirit of freedom is dead?

We all pay a price when we try to insure for
Tempestuous weather and fortune's ebb
    tide
But can you find a replacement value for
A creative soul that has withered inside?

In a cluttered world there's no longer space
    for
Vast open plains without fences and walls
But can you cage the instinctive passion for
An untamed life where wildness still calls?

Lily of the Valley

I know a secret valley
Which fire has lain bare
But contours now exposed
Still hide a beauty rare

For deep within the shadows
Beneath the silver moon
When all the earth is black
It is her time to bloom

She rises from the ashes
Laced in scarlet red
A dancing tongue of flame
Upon the valley bed

She smiles upon the landscape
As hope is rediscovered
In the midst of desolation
She's one of God's beloved.

Blue Skies

When the skies are blue
And the world is bright
I am smiling also -
Let us bask in the sunshine!

When the grey clouds come
And the sun disappears
I will be here still -
Let us hold hands in the gloom!

When the lightening strikes
And the thunderclaps rage
I will tremble also -
Let us cling tight in the storm!

When the showers fall
And the land is drenched
I too will be crying -
Let us slow dance in the rain!

When the arch unveils
And the colours enchant
I will marvel also -
Let us fly over the rainbow!

The River

Streams meet and join, then split apart
While in between, the current flows
So too with matters of the heart
Love is a tide that comes and goes

Yet even streams whose ways diverge
Are somehow always one
For waters swirl and mix and merge
And cannot be undone

And who's to say if waterfalls
Are where the river ends
Or whether, when love's river stalls,
A stream flows on as friends.

Changing Light

The crisp mauve light of morning
Of new beginnings and promises
Of kindled hope and faith
Of warm inspiration
Of sunrise

The bright white light of day-time
Of glad adventures and achievements
Of blazing love and life
Of hot dedication
Of noontide

The blood red light of evening
Of sad completion and letting go
Of parting words and ways
Of cool liberation
Of sunset

The pitch black light of night-time
Of calm reflecting and reviving
Of healing rest and care
Of cold germination
Of midnight.

I Wish I Was Lost

I wish I was lost on a beach of gold sand
Just mapless and hapless and wandering
 unplanned
With endless horizons of ocean and land
And two dreamy drifters alone hand in
 hand

I wish I was lost on a train to the sun
Just lazy and crazy and bursting with fun
With cliff-tops to climb and warnings to
 shun
And two rebel riders who've scarcely begun

I wish I was lost on a trail nowhere bound
Just blue skies and gull cries and shells on
 the ground
With wind songs and wave beats that echo
 around
And two lovers laughing in sync with the
 sound.

Season of Loving

The seasons turn –

Nature enacts her ritual of letting go

While weather-talk becomes apologetic

A procession of figures wrapped in
themselves

Begin their descent into gloomy mind-
tombs

And I prepare –

Bracing myself against the looming
darkness

Stacking reserves of emotional firewood

Battening down the hatches ready to sit
tight

Hoping that Christmas will bring more thaw
than chill

But then you came –

A Spring flower budding in my Autumn
field

A splash of colour bursting through my
grey sky

A candle flame dancing across my cave wall

A campfire raging amidst my Winter world

Now I just smile –

Knowing that there's no cold when the
    heart is warm

Trusting that there's no darkness when
    hope shines through

Feeling that Autumn and Winter are
    passing

Sensing that New Year will fulfil its
    promise.

Only Natural

Is it spoiling a rose
To breathe its sweet scent
And call its silk petals
Beautiful?

Is it blessing a tree
To stroke its rough skin
And call its bright garments
Wonderful?

Is it treating a hill
To walk its curved back
And call its wide vistas
Majestic?

Or is it we who are
Spoiled, blessed and treated
By noticing what is
Only natural?

Sliver of the Moon

Sliver of the moon
Gone too soon
Too soon gone
To the stars beyond.

The Harbour

Life's a great adventure – that's true:
You brave the storms of grey and blue
You sail across the seven seas
And chase the sunsets on the breeze

You shin the mast and touch the sky
You trim the sails and don't ask why
But just beneath the thrill and mirth
You long to find a tranquil berth

Life's a great adventure – such glee:
The ocean tells you that you're free
The salty air, the surf and spray
Add spice to every night and day

You plot the course and chart the stars
You lift the anchor, break the bars
But even as you rig and roam
You search for signs to make it home

Life's a great adventure – each day:
You're blown and buoyed along the way

You weave a yarn and tell your tale
And make a wish as you set sail

The horizon stretches as before
But now you've come to know the shore
No longer are you harbourless
What can I say: it's marvellous!

Haiku 2

Open petals glowing
With buzzing to and fro'ing
Sweet nectar's flowing.

Haiku 3

Twin swans, white as silk
Rise and fall with gentle swell
Curvatures in sync.

Safe Place

Now you're safe in your place and I'm safe
in mine

No waves and no torrents, the weather's
just fine

The distance between us keeps still waters
calm

Our harbour defences protect us from harm

But oh, how I long for the cool ocean spray

For the flap of the sails and the dolphins at
play

And oh, how I yearn for the sway of the bed

For the rap of the riggings strung tight
overhead

But I'm safe in my place and you're safe in
yours

Our anchors are dropped and we're tied to
the moors

No warnings of sea squalls, no fog horns or
bells

No risk of us sinking, no dangerous spells

Yet oh, how I miss all the wide open space

The sun on our backs and the wind in our
    face

And oh, how I dream of the day we set sail

On our next great adventure, come hell or
    high gale.

The Environmentalist

You call me an environmentalist
As if caring for the earth is some kind of
     cult
And concern for future generations
Is a subversive agenda to be treated with
     suspicion

Yet it is the earth that sustains us
And a future that we will occupy together
It is the place that all of us call home
And our children who will suffer or succeed

Being green does not make me a monster
Any more than being black or white would
In the end we all bleed the same colour
And when the earth is wounded, it bleeds
     too

You think I'm a fundamentalist
As if respect for nature is an ideology
And calling for limits to growth and
     consumption
Is propaganda with no basis in science

Yet it is nature that makes us who we are
And science that sets the conditions for life
It is a finite world that we all live in
And simple maths reveals the inconvenient
truth

Being committed does not make me a
fanatic
Any more than being a person of faith
would
In the end we all believe in something good
And when we believe in nature, it gives
back

You say I'm a conservationist
As if saving scarce resources is a bad thing
And giving space for all life to flourish
Is a zero-sum game where humans always
lose

Yet it is resources that feed and clothe us
That fuel our homes and health and
happiness
It is the web of life that supports us
And greater biodiversity means we thrive
too

Being loving does not make me weak

Any more than being a parent or saint
would

In the end we all long for compassion

And when we nurture all life, it takes care
of us

You call me an environmentalist

I confess that I am, and so much more
besides

So call me a humanist and a possible-ist
too

For I believe that a better world is possible
(do you?)